P9-CQX-899

BRITANNICA BEGINNER BIOS

ANNE FRANK

HEROIC DIARIST OF THE HOLOCAUST

HOPE LOURIE KILLCOYNE

Published in 2016 by Britannica Educational Publishing (a trademark of Encyclopædia Britannica, Inc.) in association with The Rosen Publishing Group, Inc.
29 East 21st Street, New York, NY 10010

Distributed exclusively by Rosen Publishing.
To see additional Britannica Educational Publishing titles, go to rosenpublishing.com.

First Edition

Britannica Educational Publishing
J.E. Luebering: Director, Core Reference Group
Mary Rose McCudden: Editor, Britannica Student Encyclopedia

Rosen Publishing
Philip Wolny: Editor
Nelson Sá: Art Director
Nicole Russo: Designer
Cindy Reiman: Photography Manager
Phil Wolny: Photo Researcher

Library of Congress Cataloging-in-Publication Data

Killcoyne, Hope Lourie.
Anne Frank : heroic diarist of the Holocaust/Hope Lourie Killcoyne.—First edition.
pages cm.—(Britannica beginner bios)
Includes index.
ISBN 978-1-6804-8256-0 (library bound) — ISBN 978-1-5081-0061-4 (pbk.) — ISBN 978-1-68048-314-7 (6-pack)
Frank, Anne, 1929–1945—Juvenile literature. 2. Jewish children in the Holocaust—Netherlands—Amsterdam—Biography—Juvenile literature. 3. Jews—Netherlands—Amsterdam—Biography—Juvenile literature. 4. Amsterdam (Netherlands) —Biography—Juvenile literature. I. Title.
DS135.N6F7337 2016
940.53'18092—dc23
[B]

2015022412

Manufactured in the United States of America

Photo credits: Cover, pp. 1, 6, 7, 9, 16 ullstein bild/Getty Images; p. 5 Universal Images Group/Getty Images; p. 8 Imagno/Hulton Archive/Getty Images; p. 10 Stan Honda/AFP/Getty Images; p. 11 Three Lions/Hulton Archive/Getty Images; p. 12 Everett Historical/Shutterstock; pp. 14, 19 Heritage Images/Hulton Archive/Getty Images; p. 15 AFP/Getty Images; p. 17 © Brian Harris/Alamy Stock Photo; p. 20 Bentley Archive/Popperfoto/Getty Images; p. 21 Andrew Burton/Getty Images; p. 23 PHAS/Universal Images Group/Getty3Image; p. 24 Ilia Yefimovich/Getty Images; p. 25 Rolls Press/Popperfoto/Getty Images; p. 26 Gali Tibbon/AFP/Getty Images; interior pages background image Nejron Photo/Shutterstock.com.

CONTENTS

CHAPTER ONE

THE MOST FAMOUS DIARY IN THE WORLD

Anne Frank was a Jewish girl who lived in the years right before and during World War II. It was very difficult to be Jewish in Europe at this time. Though her world became frightening and dangerous, Anne remained a happy, funny, and smart girl. She did not survive the war, but many people came to know her through a **DIARY** that she kept during those years.

Vocabulary Box

A DIARY is a notebook in which someone writes down thoughts and feelings. Some diaries, such as Anne's, include photographs.

Jewish women and children wait to enter Auschwitz, the biggest concentration camp the Germans built. More than one million people died there.

Anne's parents gave her the diary for her 13th birthday. Anne began writing about her life, her plans, and her dreams. When her diary was later published, Anne became a person many readers could relate to.

Six million Jewish men, women, and children died during World War II. Six million is such a huge number that it is hard to think about the individual victims.

A photo of Anne in her diary. As she writes, her big dream was to become a movie star.

However, Anne's diary offers a connection to one of those victims. Her thoughtful diary filled with stories and secrets, fantasies and fears, makes Anne come to life because it is the story of her life. The story becomes even more powerful because her life was cut short by the great evil that took over Europe in World War II.

CHAPTER TWO

WHAT WAS THE HOLOCAUST?

After the Nazi Party took control of Germany in 1933, Nazi leaders began to plan their invasion of other countries. In 1939 Germany invaded Poland. Poland's allies, Britain and France, then declared war on Germany, and World War II began.

Adolf Hitler led Nazi Germany from 1933 to 1945.

Germany continued to invade other countries. In 1941 the United States entered the war when Japan, Germany's ally, bombed Pearl Harbor, Hawaii. The United States, Britain, Russia, and other countries fought Germany, Japan, and Italy.

Germany's leader, Adolf Hitler, hated the Jewish people. The Nazis captured millions of Jews in Germany and the countries that they invaded, along with other

A young boy and other Jewish prisoners in Warsaw, Poland, are held at gunpoint by German soldiers.

Vocabulary Box

The HOLOCAUST was the killing of millions of European civilians during World War II. Six million Jews died, as did millions of other "undesirables," including Roma (Gypsies), the mentally and physically disabled, and political enemies of the Nazis.

By 1936 the Nazi Party controlled Germany. Here, a crowd watches a speech by Hitler in Frankfurt, the Frank family's hometown.

people they considered inferior. The end result of the Nazis' actions was the **HOLOCAUST**.

Many Jews and others were put into labor camps or concentration camps. Many in the camps were killed by guards or died from disease and starvation.

CHAPTER THREE

ESCAPE FROM GERMANY TO THE NETHERLANDS

Margot and Anne Frank are shown here with their father in 1931.

Annelies Marie Frank was born on June 12, 1929, in Frankfurt, Germany. Her parents were Otto and Edith Frank. Anne and her older sister, Margot, grew up just when anti-Jewish feeling was growing.

After the Nazi Party came to power in 1933, Otto Frank moved to the Netherlands, a small country northwest of Germany. He opened an office in the capital, Amsterdam, in September. His family joined him shortly thereafter. Anne made new friends—some Jewish, some not—and both sisters attended public school.

Nazi troops in Amsterdam, on a route from Central Station past the Queen's Palace

In May 1940, Germany invaded the Netherlands. All the Jews had to register their businesses. Later they had to give up the businesses to Gentiles (non-Jews). Otto Frank signed over his company to his business

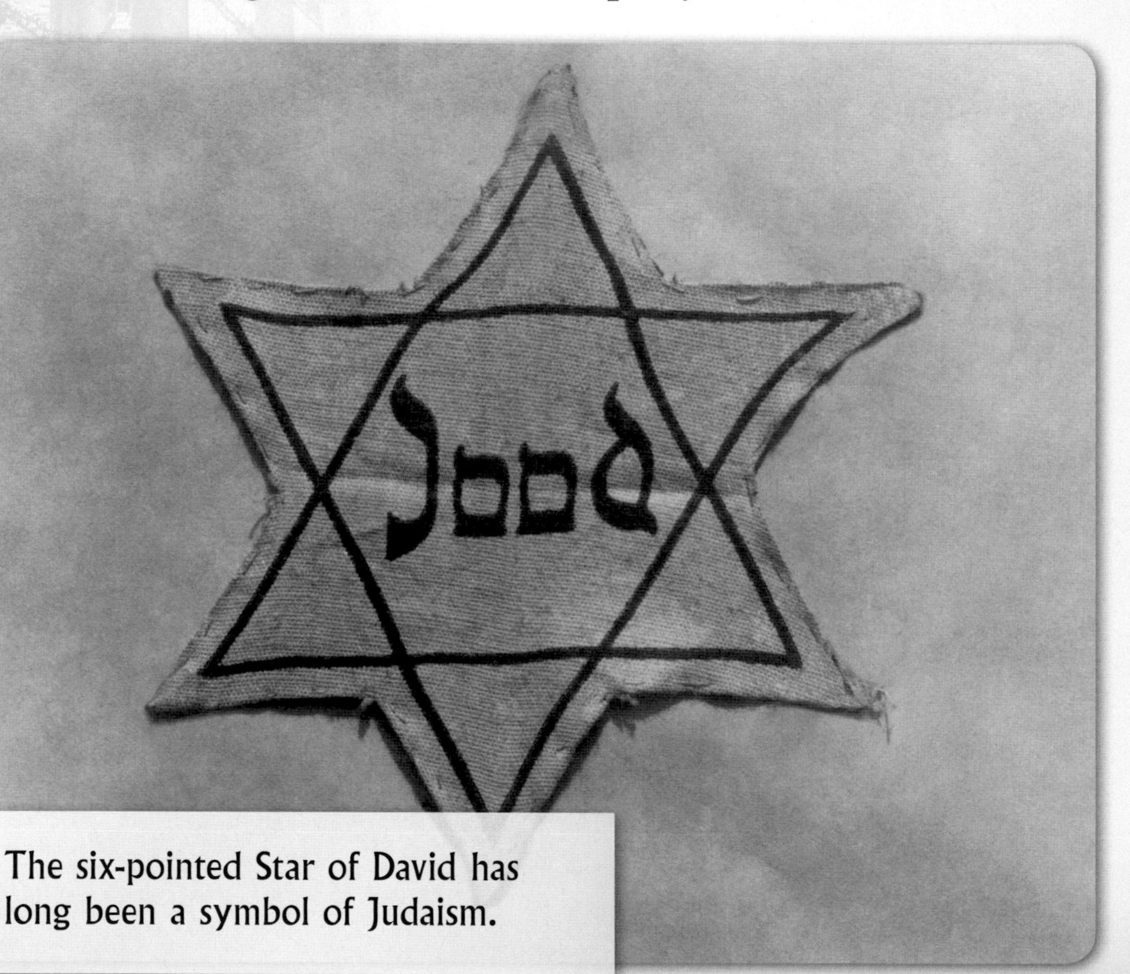

The six-pointed Star of David has long been a symbol of Judaism.

Quick Fact

The Netherlands is sometimes called Holland. Its people are the Dutch, which is also the name of their language.

partners. In 1941, the Germans began separating the Jews in the Netherlands from the rest of the population. Anne and Margot were no longer allowed to attend school with non-Jews. The Germans also started rounding up and imprisoning Jews in temporary camps.

By 1942, all Jews aged six and older had to wear a yellow Star of David on their clothes. The star was a proud religious symbol, but the Nazis had forced it on Jews as a marker of shame, to easily identify and exclude them. In the summer of 1942 the Germans began sending Jews to labor and concentration camps in other countries. Otto Frank, like many other Jews, made plans to hide his family.

CHAPTER FOUR

GOING INTO HIDING

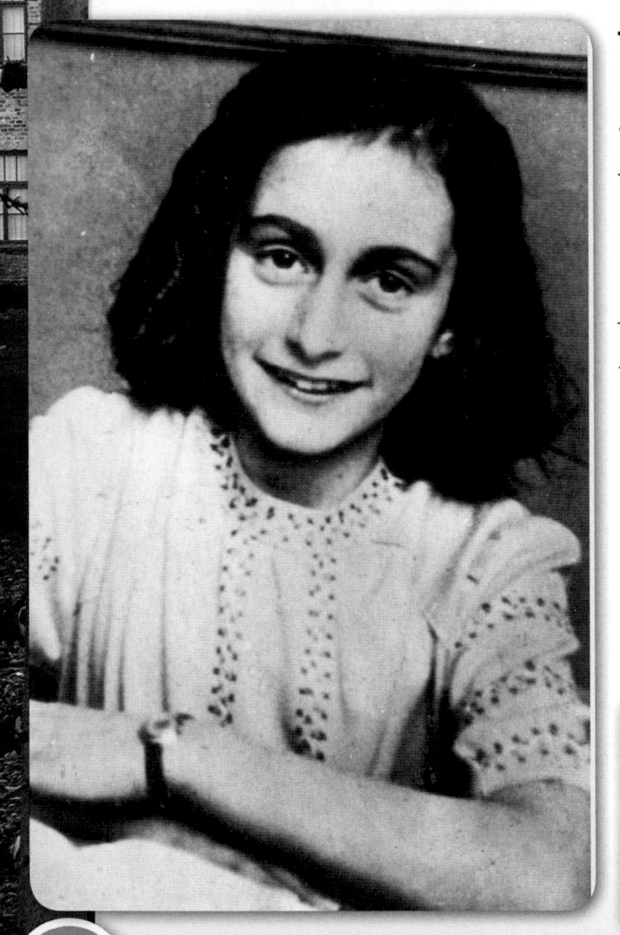

Being a teenager can be hard, but it can be even harder in wartime. The Franks received bad news on July 5, 1942, just after Anne turned 13. Margot, then 16, was notified that she had to go to a labor camp in Germany.

Luckily, Otto Frank had been preparing some rooms up-stairs from his office. This place

Anne Frank in her Amsterdam middle school, December 1941, a few months before going into hiding

Vocabulary Box

An ANNEX is an added part of a building.

would become the "secret **ANNEX**" where they could hide from the Nazis. The day after Margot got her notice, the Franks went into hiding. Another Jewish family soon joined them: Hermann and Auguste van Pels and their fifteen-year-old son, Peter. Fritz Pfeffer, another German Jew, arrived a few months later.

In hiding, Anne turned to her birthday gift: her diary. Thinking of it as a friend, she even named it: Kitty. All her entries began, "Dear Kitty."

The first thing Anne wrote to Kitty was, "I hope you will be a great support and comfort to me."

Several of Otto's employees helped the Franks and the others in the annex. A woman named Miep Gies and others brought them food, supplies, and news of the outside world. The entrance to the annex was a door concealed by a bookcase. Miep and the few other employees were the only ones who knew about the annex.

Miep Gies, seen here in 1994, became a close, trusted friend and protector of the Frank family.

Life in the Annex

For more than two years, the Franks tiptoed around during daytime. They feared that someone downstairs might hear them and betray them. Meanwhile, the eight captives tried to lead as normal a life as possible. Anne, Margot, and Peter studied and did homework. At

The bookcase swung open and led into the annex hiding place.

night, when the business shut down, they listened to the news on the radio.

Anne told Kitty about the ups and downs of life in hiding. She was honest about the others and herself. Somehow, she held onto her optimism about the future and her belief in the goodness of people. She wrote, "In spite of everything I still believe that people are really good at heart."

Throughout 1944, the people in hiding became hopeful that the Nazis would be defeated soon. But on August 4, 1944, a group led by Karl Silberbauer, an investigator in the Gestapo (the German secret police), raided the annex based on an informant's tip. Anne and the rest were arrested and sent away.

Quick Fact

Otto Frank was the only resident of the annex to survive the Holocaust.

Eventually, they were taken to Auschwitz, Nazi Germany's largest death camp, located in Poland. While there, Edith Frank died of starvation. In October, Anne and Margot were taken from Auschwitz to the Bergen-Belsen concentration camp in Germany. The living conditions there were horrible, and they became sick, probably from

The Austrian police officer Karl Silberbauer was revealed years later to be the leader of the group that arrested the residents of the secret annex.

British soldiers arrested Josef Kramer, commanding officer of the Bergen-Belsen camp.

the then often deadly infection known as typhus. Anne and Margot died in February or March 1945. Weeks later, on April 15, British soldiers freed the camp's prisoners.

CHAPTER FIVE

ANNE'S DIARY, HER HOUSE, HER LEGACY

After the annex was raided, Miep Gies found Anne's diary and other pages scattered on the floor. She took them all, hoping to return everything to Anne.

Here is the original cover of the 1947 edition of Anne Frank's account. The title can be translated as *The Annex: Diary Notes from 12 June 1942 to 1 August 1944.*

Russian troops freed survivors at

Auschwitz in January 1945, including Otto Frank. He spent six months making his way back to the Netherlands. It turned out he was the only survivor of their wartime hiding place.

When Miep Gies learned that Anne had died, she gave the diary to Otto. He transcribed (rewrote) and translated it from Dutch for relatives in Switzerland. He realized Anne's thoughts and experiences during the war would be important for others to read. A historian helped Otto Frank with the manuscript. Otto finally published Anne's diary in 1947. Eventually, it was translated into more than 65 languages and became one of the world's most widely read books.

Quick Fact

More than a million people visit the Anne Frank House every year. It is one of the most visited museums in the Netherlands.

In 1957, when the annex was about to be torn down, many people joined together to save the space. It was made into a museum: the Anne Frank House.

Today, visitors to the Anne Frank House go past the door-like bookcase, up steep steps to where the Franks and their friends lived. None of the rooms contain furniture except for

The exterior of the Anne Frank House in the modern era is shown here.

whatever could not be removed, such as the stove and sinks. In another part of the building are exhibit rooms with diary quotes, filmstrips, and photos from Anne's life hung on the walls. Anne's original diary is permanently on display in the museum as well. Visitors can see pages of the diary and learn more about her life and tragic death.

The Anne Frank House has exhibits about the war and allows visitors to see Anne's diary.

A Legacy of Hope and Tolerance

The Anne Frank House does not let visitors leave over-come with sadness. With the wisdom and kindness of

Otto Frank shows the annex entrance to Queen Juliana of the Netherlands on the 50th anniversary of Anne Frank's birth.

Anne herself, the final exhibit provides escape. How? In the last room, museum-goers take part in a question-and-answer session. There, they answer yes or no to

Holocaust survivor Hanna Pick (*left*), a friend of Anne's, plants a tree with her granddaughter Tamar Meir (*center*) next to the Yad Vashem Holocaust Memorial in Jerusalem, Israel, on March 26, 2012.

modern-day questions about personal freedoms such as wearing head scarves, religious jewelry, and even Nazi-type clothing in public. This process allows the heart to rest while the brain takes over.

The museum also helps visitors think a bit more deeply about intolerance and persecution in today's world. Many people around the world continue to suffer exclusion, mistrust, or hatred every day because they are different in some way from others around them. In some places, women and girls are not given the same rights as men. In other places, people are mistreated because of their religion, nationality, or behavior.

The museum and the diary continue to inspire interest in Anne's life. They also continue to teach people about the Holocaust. Anne's legacy is one of hope and humanity in the face of fear and evil.

TIMELINE

1929: Annelies Marie Frank is born in Frankfurt, Germany. Margot Frank is three years old.

1933: Austrian-born Adolf Hitler becomes the leader of Germany.

Otto and Edith Frank, Anne and Margot's parents, move the family to Amsterdam in the Netherlands, where they believe that they will be safer.

1934: Anne and Margot attend public Dutch school. Anne will stay at the school until 1941.

1937: The van Pels family make their escape from Germany to the Netherlands.

1938: In a horrible event known as the Night of Broken Glass, more than 1,000 Jewish synagogues (temples) and more than 7,000 Jewish-owned shops in Germany and Austria are burned and destroyed, the windows shattered. About 30,000 Jewish teenagers and men are arrested and sent to concentration camps. In order to hold so many new prisoners, several camps have to be made bigger.

Fritz Pfeffer flees Berlin, Germany, for Amsterdam.

1939: Germany invades Poland. World War II begins.

1940: Germany invades the Netherlands, Belgium, and France. Jews are no longer allowed to own businesses. Otto Frank appoints his non-Jewish partner as director.

1941: Germans began separating the Jews in the Netherlands from the rest of the population.

1942: Jews in Germany and all the countries Germany invaded must now wear a yellow Jewish star on their clothing.

The Franks and their friends go into hiding in the annex.

Anne writes: "Not being able to go outside upsets me more than I can say, and I'm terrified our hiding place will be discovered and that we'll be shot."

1944: The hideaways are discovered, arrested, and sent to Auschwitz.

American forces arrive in Paris and liberate (free) the French capital from German rule.

Hermann van Pels is sent to the gas chambers at Auschwitz in autumn.

Fritz Pfeffer, being moved from one camp to another, becomes ill and dies in December.

1945: Edith Frank sees her daughters taken away from Auschwitz. She dies in January 1945.

1945: Margot and Anne Frank catch a disease called typhus. They die, most likely in February.

Peter van Pels, exhausted by the work he is doing while in a labor camp, dies in April or May. His mother dies around the same time.

Hitler kills himself on April 30. Germany surrenders on May 8.

Otto Frank returns to Amsterdam. Not yet knowing that he is the only survivor of the annex, he places an advertisement in the paper trying to find his daughters. Soon afterward, he meets two sisters who saw Anne and Margot die.

1947: Anne's diary is published for the first time. Her father says, "If she had been here, Anne would have been so proud."

1955: A play based on the events recorded in the diary is performed for the first time.

1959: A film version of the play is released.

1960: The Anne Frank House opens to the public.

GLOSSARY

CAPTIVE Someone who is not free to leave.

CONCENTRATION CAMP A prison camp where many people are held in a small space and where they are forced to work or are housed until being executed.

GESTAPO The German secret police that operated behind the scenes within Germany and Germany-occupied territories.

INFORMANT Someone who gives information in order to accuse or cause suspicion.

INVADED Entered and took over, such as an army from one country taking over another country.

MANUSCRIPT The handwritten or typed version of a written work, before it is printed or published.

OPTIMISM A habit of expecting everything to turn out for the best.

PERSECUTION Treatment of people that is meant to be cruel and harmful and to cause suffering.

TRANSCRIBE To make a copy of a handwritten text into a typed work.

UNDESIRABLES People who are unwanted and who are seen as being less than human.

FOR MORE INFORMATION

BOOKS

Frank, Anne. *Anne Frank: The Diary of a Young Girl.* New York, NY: Bantam Books, 1993.

Metselaar, Menno, and Ruud van der Rol. *Anne Frank: Her Life in Words and Pictures from the Archives of the Anne Frank House.* New York, NY: Roaring Brook Press, 2009.

Waxman, Laura Hamilton. *Anne Frank*. Minneapolis, MN: Lerner Publications Company, 2009.

Zapruder, Alexandra. *National Geographic Readers: Anne Frank*. Washington, DC: National Geographic Society, 2013.

WEBSITES

Because of the changing nature of Internet links, Rosen Publishing has developed an online list of websites related to the subject of this book. This site is updated regularly. Please use this link to access this list:

http://www.rosenlinks.com/BBB/Frank